The Science of Vaccines

Don Nardo

ReferencePoint Press®

San Diego, CA

About the Author

Classical historian, amateur astronomer, and award-winning author Don Nardo has written numerous volumes about scientific topics, including *Destined for Space*, winner of the Eugene M. Emme Award for best astronomical literature; *Tycho Brahe*, winner of the National Science Teaching Association's best book of the year; *Planet Under Siege*; *Climate Change*; *Deadliest Dinosaurs*; and *The History of Science*. Nardo, who also composes and arranges orchestral music, lives with his wife, Christine, in Massachusetts.

© 2022 ReferencePoint Press, Inc.
Printed in the United States

For more information, contact:
ReferencePoint Press, Inc.
PO Box 27779
San Diego, CA 92198
www.ReferencePointPress.com

ALL RIGHTS RESERVED.
No part of this work covered by the copyright hereon may be reproduced or used in any form or by any means—graphic, electronic, or mechanical, including photocopying, recording, taping, web distribution, or information storage retrieval systems—without the written permission of the publisher.

LIBRARY OF CONGRESS CATALOGING-IN-PUBLICATION DATA

Names: Nardo, Don, 1947- author.
Title: The science of vaccines / by Don Nardo.
Description: San Diego, CA : ReferencePoint Press, 2022. | Series:
   Understanding infectious diseases | Includes bibliographical references
   and index.
Identifiers: LCCN 2021003833 (print) | LCCN 2021003834 (ebook) | ISBN
   9781678201623 (library binding) | ISBN 9781678201630 (ebook)
Subjects: LCSH: Vaccines--History--Juvenile literature. |
   Vaccinations--History--Juvenile literature. | COVID-19--Juvenile
   literature.
Classification: LCC QR189 .N364 2022 (print) | LCC QR189 (ebook) | DDC
   615.3/72--dc23
LC record available at https://lccn.loc.gov/2021003833
LC ebook record available at https://lccn.loc.gov/2021003834

CONTENTS

A Moon Landing for Modern Medicine

Medical experts worldwide agree that the period spanning late 2020 through early 2021 will be remembered as one of the most consequential in the history of modern science. On the one hand, during those fateful months COVID-19, a devastating, contagious disease characterized by acute respiratory difficulties, raged across the globe. It had emerged in rural China in December 2019 and from there spread rapidly to nearly every nation on earth. Claiming several thousand victims each day, by mid-February 2021 COVID-19 had numbered some 27 million confirmed cases and had caused roughly 475,000 deaths in the United States alone. At that moment, worldwide cases numbered 108 million and the global death count for the disease was 2.4 million.

Even more significant, but in a far more positive way, in late 2020 news agencies around the world announced what many observers called a medical miracle. Multiple vaccines designed to fight back against COVID-19 had been approved for use. Most often injected through a shot in the arm, a vaccine is a human-made substance that induces the body to become resistant, or even immune, to a given disease.

Among the many experts who hailed the COVID-19 vaccines' emergence was US Food and Drug Administration (FDA) commissioner Stephen M. Hahn, who called it a "significant milestone" in medical research. He continued, "The tireless work to develop a new vaccine to prevent this novel, serious, and life threatening disease in an expedited time frame after its emergence is a true testament to scientific innovation and public-private collaboration worldwide."[1]

A Scientific Triumph

Hahn's words "in an expedited time frame" are the key to understanding why the development of these vaccines was such a historic achievement. Usually, it takes years rather than months to create a new vaccine. "Most vaccines have taken decades to develop,"[2] American microbiologist Eric J. Rubin remarked in late 2020. He and other researchers have pointed out that before COVID-19 arrived on the scene, the development of the mumps vaccine was widely viewed as lightning fast. That vaccine was introduced in 1967 after four years in development. But as Rubin says, the initial COVID-19 vaccines moved "from conception to large-scale implementation within a year." In the annals of modern medicine, he adds, "this is a triumph."[3]

vaccine

A human-made substance that induces the body to become resistant, or even immune, to a given disease

One reason that vaccines typically take so long to create is that researchers want to make sure they are safe for use on hundreds of thousands, or even millions, of people. So it is routine to demand that a new vaccine undergo rigorous testing. Much of this takes the form of a series of trials in which living things are injected with the vaccine and their reactions carefully monitored. Most of the time the trials occur in at least four phases, the first consisting of tests on animals such as rats and chimps.

Assuming the animal testing goes smoothly, three phases of human trials generally follow. The first determines whether the vaccine is safe for small groups of people; in the second phase, researchers establish the safest and most effective doses; and

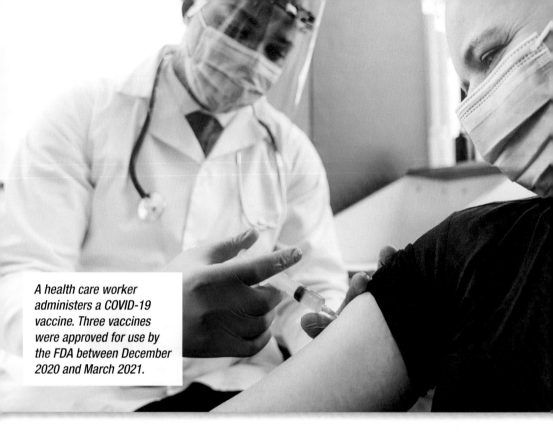

A health care worker administers a COVID-19 vaccine. Three vaccines were approved for use by the FDA between December 2020 and March 2021.

the third phase finds out whether the vaccine is safe to use on the general population. If the vaccine passes all three human trials without any major adverse effects, the government licenses it for distribution to the public.

A Staggering Amount of Money

Usually, all those steps take at least a few years to accomplish, partly because they are very complex and expensive to administer. Most often a single company is developing the vaccine and has only so much development money at its disposal. The case of the search for COVID-19 vaccines was different because the pandemic rather suddenly struck on a global scale and swiftly killed huge numbers of people. Prompted by widespread fear, more than a dozen countries had labs that were already working on vaccines by February 2020. By September of that same year, almost one hundred more labs in multiple countries had joined the search.

Furthermore, the amount of money involved was simply staggering. A 2018 study reported in the *Lancet Global Health* medical journal estimated that the development of a single vaccine typically costs $30 million to $68 million. That is a lot of money, to be sure. But it pales before the global funding for COVID-19 vaccines. European governments and research organizations alone pledged more than $8 billion to the search for a COVID-19 vaccine. Meanwhile, the US government and various wealthy American investors raised well over $10 billion.

With access to funds of that amount, researchers around the world were able to outfit their labs with state-of-the-art equipment and hire many of the best scientists. The result was a full-scale, unprecedented assault on the virus. "By investing in multiple companies and vaccine platforms at once," says Eric J. Yager, who teaches microbiology at the Albany College of Pharmacy, researchers "increased the odds of having a vaccine, or vaccines, available by the beginning of 2021."[4] Also, Yager points out, there was a remarkably high interest in the vaccine trials by volunteers from all walks of life. With so many people willing to risk their lives in order to test the new vaccines, the trials went far faster than usual.

Thus, in late December 2020, COVID-19 vaccines produced by the pharmaceutical giant Pfizer and a smaller company, Moderna (based in Cambridge, Massachusetts), began to be administered in the United States and a few other countries. This was only ten months after COVID-19 started its destructive march across the continents. Yager calls it an amazing series of events that for modern medicine is like the "landing on the moon moment"[5] was for the science of space exploration.

CHAPTER ONE

How the Vaccine Workhorses Fight Disease

"I was so scared to lose my daughter," Yemeni mother Salwah Abdullah told a United Nations (UN) official in mid-2018. "I would have given my own life to save her."[6] A few months earlier, Salwah's daughter, Selwan, had come down with a number of gruesome and scary symptoms, including frequent vomiting and repeated bouts of severe diarrhea. After examining Selwan, local medical personnel informed her mother that the young woman, then twenty, had contracted the deadly waterborne disease cholera. This was not surprising, because in 2017 Yemen, an impoverished nation situated in the southern sector of the Arabian Peninsula, was gripped by one of the biggest cholera epidemics of the modern era. More than 1 million Yemeni perished before the UN agency UNICEF and the World Health Organization (WHO) brought the crisis under control.

In addition to helping farmers and other Yemeni citizens learn how to clean up water supplies contaminated with cholera germs, UNICEF and WHO vaccinated more than 270,000 people in only a few months. They administered one of three cholera vaccines shown to be effective against that dreaded ailment. It was too late for Selwan to get the vaccine, since she had already come down with the disease. Fortunately for the Abdullah family, however, WHO-trained nurses in a Yemeni clinic gave Selwan round-the-clock care, and she survived her bout with cholera. Most others in her village, however, did receive the vaccine, and as a result few of them got the disease. Thankful for the vaccine program that saved her neighbors, Selwan told the UN official, "I am dreaming of a Yemen free of diseases and epidemics."[7]

Few Yemeni were familiar with vaccines before the massive cholera vaccination program began in their country. The members of the Abdullah family and their neighbors and friends learned a great deal about modern medicine during those months. In particular, they were told that a vaccine gives the body protection against a given disease by triggering the body's natural immune system. Moreover, it provides that lifesaving protection without introducing the disease itself. According to WHO, "Vaccines work by training and preparing the body's natural defenses—the immune system—to recognize and fight off the viruses and bacteria they target. If the body is exposed to those disease-causing germs later, the body is immediately ready to destroy them, preventing illness."[8]

Dependable Live Vaccines

Since the 1800s scientists have developed several different kinds of vaccines that have proved to be effective. Some experts refer to them as the workhorses, or reliable mainstays, of modern medicine's vaccine arsenal. All work by stimulating immunity to disease, but each accomplishes that goal in a somewhat different manner.

The first of the workhorse vaccines to be developed, and still among the most effective, are known in scientific terms as live and attenuated. They are "live" in the sense that they consist of the actual germs of the disease one wants to fight and are still alive when injected into a person. Yet they are not normal, full-strength germs when they enter the body. Instead, they are "attenuated," or weakened, by subjecting them to heat and/or other artificial processes in a lab. The weakened form of the disease is not strong enough to cause the person to get sick, but it does stimulate the body to form an immune response, or protection, against that harmful germ.

attenuation

The process of weakening a disease germ to make it safe for use in a vaccine

The specific way this works can be seen by examining one of the diseases for which scientists most commonly use live attenuation in making vaccines to fight them. Among these ailments are cholera, yellow fever, chicken pox, and measles. Cholera, for instance, which affected so many people in Yemen in 2017–2018, attacks the intestines, often causing diarrhea. In cases where the latter becomes severe, there is a major loss of fluids that can make the victim go into shock and possibly die.

To make the live attenuated cholera vaccine, technicians first carefully grow cholera germs in a controlled manner in a lab container—a process called culturing. Next they employ either heat or a chemical (or in some cases both) to the culture in or-

In 2017 in the impoverished nation of Yemen, a young boy fills a container with well water. International observers feared that most of that country's wells had been contaminated by deadly cholera germs.

der to weaken those microbes. The weakened germs are mixed with other chemicals, along with some harmless fluids, and that mixture—the vaccine—is ready to be injected into a patient.

After the injection, the body detects the cholera germs, and the immune system sends antibodies, or soldier cells, to attack them. After the already weakened cholera germs have been destroyed, something crucial occurs. Namely, the person's immune system remembers the characteristics of the cholera bacterium, and if that person is ever again exposed to the germ, his or her body will automatically and very quickly send cholera-targeted antibodies to the infection site. Once vaccinated, therefore, that individual is immune to cholera.

antibodies

Soldier cells the immune system sends to fight invading germs

Killed Vaccines

Live attenuated vaccines have long proved to be dependable and effective against a number of harmful diseases. However, early in the history of vaccine development, scientists recognized a small downside to this type of vaccine. It was that even though the disease germs in such a vaccine have been weakened in the lab, they are still alive. For that reason, there remains a tiny yet ever-present chance that the recipient of the vaccine might end up contracting the disease. If so, however, it will not be a full-blown version of the infection. The American Academy of Allergy, Asthma, and Immunology explains that it is typically a very "mild case of the disease. Chickenpox vaccine, for example, can cause a child to develop a rash, but only with a few spots [and] this isn't harmful."[9]

Nevertheless, as time went on, medical researchers strove to create vaccines with zero chance of causing infection. The first successful version was and still is known as a killed, or inactivated, vaccine. In this kind of vaccine, the disease germs are not merely weakened but instead, as the name indicates, are killed in the lab by dousing them with chemicals or radiation

A Vaccine for Every Illness?

As the longtime scourge of malaria stands near the brink of eradication, or at least becoming a rare occurrence, it is only natural to examine a question often asked about vaccines. Namely, why have scientists not yet developed vaccines for *all* harmful diseases? After all, vaccine technology, including that of the workhorses and some new, emerging techniques, has advanced by leaps and bounds in recent decades.

The answer to that haunting question is twofold. First, some diseases have built-in strengths that traditional vaccines cannot yet overcome. One major example is the process of mutation, in which germs change into new versions of themselves too quickly and too often for new vaccines to keep pace with them. There is no universal flu vaccine, for instance, because that illness mutates too rapidly. So a new vaccine must be produced for each mutation. HIV/AIDS is another example. *New York Times* science reporter Donald G. McNeil Jr. points out that HIV "mutates as fast in one day as flu does in a year." The second reason that many serious diseases have no vaccine yet is because developing them is enormously expensive, and the sad fact is that not enough funding exists to develop them all.

Donald G. McNeil Jr., "Why Don't We Have Vaccines Against Everything?," *New York Times*, November 19, 2018. www.nytimes.com.

they cannot withstand. This process renders them completely harmless to animals and people.

Yet even though they have been deactivated, the dead germs are capable of stimulating immunity when used in a vaccine. This is because the "corpses" of those microbes retain certain physical features that the body's soldier cells can detect. Once identified by those protective cells, the dead germs in a sense enter the immune system's memory bank, and the person becomes immune to the disease.

One small disadvantage of killed vaccines is that the immunity they create is weaker than that created by live vaccines. Thus, although killed vaccines are safer than live ones, they produce a shorter period of immunity. For that reason, in most cases the vaccinated individual needs to receive one or more extra injections, called booster shots. These ensure that the immunity to the disease in question remains active.

This is why the vaccines for rabies, polio, and hepatitis A—all made with killed germs—require boosters. In fact, booster shots can in some cases mark the difference between life and death. Rabies, one of the deadliest of all diseases, is a good example. The world-famous Mayo Clinic advises:

> Once a rabies infection is established, there's no effective treatment. Though a small number of people have survived rabies, the disease usually causes death. For that reason . . . if you've been bitten by an animal that is known to have rabies, you'll receive a series of shots to prevent the rabies virus from infecting you. If the animal that bit you can't be found, it may be safest to assume that the animal has rabies.[10]

Vaccines That Fight Against Toxins

During the decades in which the first killed vaccines were under development, researchers found that disease microbes are not the only microscopic agents that can make people and animals ill. In some cases, they discovered, the culprits are secretions, or discharges, given off by the germs. These secretions, which are poisonous, are called toxins. Among the sicknesses caused by toxins are tetanus, whooping cough, diphtheria, and botulism.

Not surprisingly, when researchers began working on vaccines to combat those ailments, they named them antitoxin, or toxoid, vaccines. The first such illness that scientists tried to eradicate with a toxoid vaccine was diphtheria. A serious respiratory condition, it is characterized by lung congestion, fever, internal bleeding, and nerve destruction and in a fairly high proportion of cases can end in death. Europe, Asia, and North America all experienced diphtheria epidemics in past ages. Indeed, before 1942, when a toxoid vaccine for the disease went into wide use, the United States had many years in which over one hundred thousand cases and more than ten thousand deaths from that illness were reported.

In their approach to making toxoid vaccines to reduce those scary figures, scientists began by injecting guinea pigs with tiny amounts of live diphtheria germs. As expected, once in the animals' systems, those microbes secreted toxins into their bloodstreams. To help fight those toxins, the guinea pigs' immune systems produced specific antibodies called antitoxins.

Next the researchers drained fluid containing the antitoxins from the guinea pigs and injected it into lab animals that had not been exposed to diphtheria. Just as the scientists had hoped, the antitoxins from the guinea pigs stimulated immunity to the disease in the second group of animals. Thereafter, researchers used a similar approach to create a toxoid diphtheria vaccine in animals for use on humans. Sure enough, in the years following the vaccine's widespread application, the disease became exceedingly rare. Subsequently, it was common in the United States for fewer than five or six people to contract diphtheria annually, and from 2004 to 2008 zero US cases were reported.

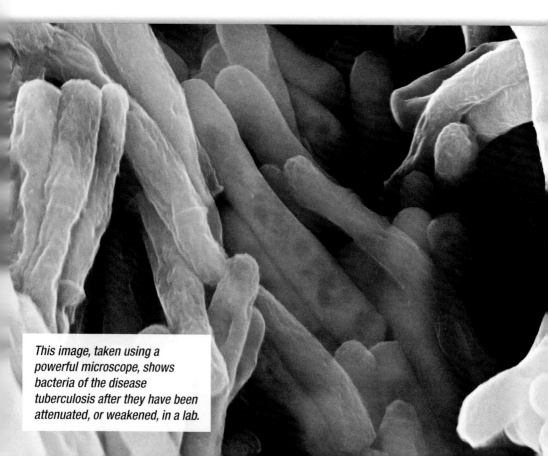

This image, taken using a powerful microscope, shows bacteria of the disease tuberculosis after they have been attenuated, or weakened, in a lab.

Why It Is So Hard to Make an AIDS Vaccine

Despite decades of trying, researchers have not yet managed to create an effective vaccine for HIV/AIDS. One reason is that the virus mutates extremely rapidly into slightly different versions of itself. Another and very crucial reason it is so hard to make an AIDS vaccine is that, unlike the situation with most other diseases, HIV actually attacks the immune system. This hampers the body's ability to muster a standard immune response. According to WebMD, an online site in which physicians explain health-related issues to the public:

> Your immune system has many types of white blood cells that fight infection. HIV gets inside a kind called CD4 cells and makes copies of itself. The virus kills the cell, and the new viruses go off to find more. Your body responds by making more CD4 cells, but after a while, it can't keep up with the virus. This makes your immune system weak. You're more likely to get sick, even from common germs. Infections last longer, are more severe, and might come back more often.

WebMD, "Effects of HIV on the Body," 2019. www.webmd.com.

Diphtheria is not as rare in some other countries as it is in the United States, however. Moreover, it is possible for Americans who travel to nations where periodic outbreaks of the disease occur to contract it and bring it with them when they return home. In 2003, for example, an American man visited the island nation of Haiti, where hundreds of diphtheria cases occur each year. On his return home he began showing symptoms of the illness, and seventeen days later, despite receiving treatment in a hospital, he died. Medical investigators found that he had received the diphtheria toxoid vaccine as a child but had not had any boosters in later years. (Like killed vaccines, toxoid ones often require booster shots.) Hoping to avoid more such tragedies, UN health authorities have frequently repeated the following warning in recent years: "It is recommended that national authorities remind travelers going to areas with diphtheria outbreaks to be properly vaccinated prior to travel in accordance with the national vaccination scheme established in each country. If more than five years have passed since their last dose, a booster dose is recommended."[11]

Synthetic Subunit Vaccines

Still another class of the workhorse vaccines developed in the past century and a half uses neither whole germs (whether alive or killed) or the secretions they give off. Instead, the vaccines in this category employ small parts, or individual units, of germs and for that reason are generally called "subunit vaccines." They have proved effective against a variety of illnesses, including hepatitis B, influenza (the "flu"), and human papillomavirus (HPV).

One of the most versatile of the subunit vaccines is called the synthetic peptide. In this case the key word is *synthetic*, meaning "artificial or human-made," so named because this type of vaccine seeks to fool the immune system into acting as if something artificial is natural. More specifically, the strategy is to make a person's body respond as though a full-fledged disease germ is attacking, when in actuality it is not, and thus muster antibodies to fight it.

subunit vaccine

A vaccine that employs a small part, or unit, of a disease germ rather than the entire microbe

To make such a vaccine, researchers first culture germs of the disease they want to fight. Then, using a microscope, they find and isolate the part of the germ's outer shell that is most likely to trigger an immune response in the human body. In the case of certain diseases, that very small part of the microbe is called a peptide. After studying the peptide in great detail, the scientists synthesize, or manufacture, a copy of it by combining molecules of a number of lab chemicals. The intent is to inject this synthetic protein into a person's body, where the immune system will respond as if real germs are attacking, mount a defense, and thereby build up immunity to that disease.

The Scourge of Malaria

Subunit vaccines have proved effective against viruses like those that cause the flu. Viruses are extremely tiny germs—in fact, the smallest known to exist. However, the subunit approach to making vaccines has shown no less promise for combating the largest disease germs known. Called protozoa, they are complex parasitic microbes that cause several harmful diseases, including malaria, sleeping sickness, and amoebic dysentery.

For a long time scientists hoped to make a malaria vaccine, but attempts to do so using live attenuated and killed germs failed. This was worrisome because each year that illness, which causes fever, vomiting, and extreme weakness, infects close to 300 million people and kills roughly 1 million of them. Finally, in 2019 the first major antimalaria vaccine began large-scale human trials in the African nations of Kenya, Ghana, and Malawi. Developed by an alliance of global companies (including London-based GlaxoSmithKline) and government agencies, it is a subunit

In 2019, mothers and their young children in the African nation of Malawi take part in a large-scale human trial of the new malaria vaccine conducted in that and some neighboring countries.

vaccine that employs a specific protein found on the surface of the malaria protozoan.

Enthusiastic about the future prospects of the vaccine, as the trials began, a WHO official commented, "The malaria vaccine has the potential to save tens of thousands of children's lives."[12] Lelio Marmora, of the global health organization Unitaid, agreed and said, "The malaria vaccine is an exciting innovation that complements the global health community's efforts to end the malaria epidemic. It is also a shining example of the kind of inter-agency coordination that we need."[13]

Traditional approaches to making subunit vaccines have used particles—like the protein in the malaria vaccine—that exist on a virus's outer surface. But what about the tiny units lurking deep inside the microbe? Today researchers are also delving into the shadowy world of the individual genes that make those microscopic organisms what they are. In so doing they have pioneered an exciting new path to immunity—the realm of genetic vaccines.

CHAPTER TWO

Vaccines on the Cutting Edge

On a Sunday afternoon in early November 2020, vaccine researcher Barney Graham received a call from his boss at the National Institutes of Health, in Bethesda, Maryland. For almost the entire ten months leading up to that day, Graham had diligently worked with his colleagues, intent on developing a vaccine to make people immune to COVID-19—the disease that was spreading around the world and killing hundreds of thousands of people.

In that call, Graham learned something exciting about the vaccine that was developed by the large pharmaceutical company Pfizer and had been in human trials for a few weeks. That vaccine, his boss said, was proving more effective than even the most optimistic scientists had hoped. Both men were elated because they had recently helped design a new vaccine technology and had given it to Pfizer, as well as to Moderna, a Massachusetts-based company that had also created a COVID-19 vaccine.

The techniques Graham and his coworkers had developed centered on a kind of genetic material called messenger RNA, usually abbreviated as mRNA. As explained by *Washington Post* science reporter Carolyn Y. Johnson, mRNA is the microscopic substance "that makes life possible, taking the instructions inscribed in DNA and delivering those to the protein-making parts of the cell. Messenger RNA is a powerful [component] of life's building blocks."[14]

mRNA

Stands for "messenger RNA," the genetic material that delivers instructions from DNA to the body's cells

Scientists had known about mRNA for several decades, but most of them did not think it showed any promise for vaccine development. A few, like Graham and his colleagues, disagreed. So when COVID-19 began ravaging the world, they wisely moved forward with research to explore mRNA as a potential resource for making vaccines. "The world faced an unparalleled threat," Johnson writes, and some companies, including Pfizer and Moderna "leaped into the fight" wielding mRNA. Thanks to these vaccines, says Johnson, millions of people will survive and will owe their existence to a few courageous scientists "who pursued ideas they thought were important even when the world doubted them."[15]

A New Branch of Vaccine Technology

Even though mRNA had never been used to make vaccines, scientists had long recognized that it might be possible to use other genetic materials for that purpose. The new branch of vaccine technology that seeks to employ those materials began in earnest in the early 1980s. Researchers at the New York State Department of Health devised a strategy, or general approach, for making subunit vaccines using DNA molecules as the fundamental units.

DNA, which stands for deoxyribonucleic acid, is a large, complex molecule that contains the microscopic particles called genes. They carry the instructions for the growth and functioning of all living things, including most germs. In 1953 scientists James Watson and Francis Crick discovered and described the structure of DNA. They showed that each DNA molecule is shaped like a spiral staircase and that the genes are lined up beside one another in the long strands making up each tiny staircase.

On the one hand, knowing about the structure of DNA allowed scientists to better understand how genetic information passes from parents to their children. On the other hand, more

In 1953, scientists James Watson (left) and Francis Crick (right) stand beside a large-scale model of the spiral structure of the DNA molecule they had recently discovered.

specifically regarding vaccines, immunologists realized that certain genes might possibly be used as the central particles in new approaches to subunit vaccines. In one approach, researchers could in theory isolate a given gene existing inside a disease germ. Perhaps, advocates of this idea hypothesized, those tiny pieces of genetic material from the inner structure of a disease microbe could signal the immune system to create germ-fighting soldier cells to fight against that illness.

Using those basic ideas as guidelines, researchers developed an overall theoretical approach to making DNA vaccines. It consists of first selecting and isolating a tiny piece of DNA from a harmless germ. The scientists then use genetic engineering techniques to alter that particle, making it resemble a similar unit in a harmful disease microbe. The transformed particle is next injected directly into human cells. When the altered genetic unit enters a cell, some of its components move to the nucleus, or center. In response—as if the harmless particle is an invading disease

A Breakthrough in Cancer Vaccines

Researchers have been trying to develop DNA-based vaccines to fight cancer for over two decades. No anticancer vaccine has yet been licensed, in part because a number of technical problems still need to be overcome. One of these difficulties is the fact that so far most of the experimental vaccines have targeted healthy cells as well as cancerous ones. In 2020 scientists working at Washington University School of Medicine, in St. Louis, Missouri, announced that they had isolated a protein fragment that has the potential to make vaccines that will attack only unhealthy tissue. According to Julia Evangelou Strait, a member of the National Association of Science Writers:

> The mutated DNA of cancer cells often produces abnormal proteins, whose fragments can help distinguish the tumor from healthy tissue. Such protein fragments could be harnessed to train the immune system to attack the tumors with, in theory, few side effects. Now, a broad collaboration of scientists in academia and industry have identified the most important features of the protein fragments to help researchers design better immunotherapies against cancer.

Julia Evangelou Strait, "New Discovery Could Help Improve Cancer Vaccines," Washington University School of Medicine, October 9, 2020. https://medicine.wustl.edu.

germ—the immune system goes to work, and soon the person is protected against the targeted disease.

Partly as a result of the enormous complexity of DNA and the huge number of genes, proteins, and other particles it contains, progress in developing DNA vaccines has been slow. As of 2021 the only versions licensed for use were veterinary, or specifically engineered to make animals immune to diseases that affect only them. Nevertheless, numerous labs around the globe continue to search for new DNA vaccines to fight maladies that affect humans. Among others, they include anthrax, rabies, malaria, hepatitis C, HPV, and cancer.

Potential Advantages of DNA Vaccines

Although vaccines for some of those illnesses already exist, scientists hope to supplement the existing vaccines with newer, cutting edge DNA versions. This is because they believe that DNA-based vaccines will have certain advantages over more conventional varieties. One such advantage is faster and stronger protection, says VGXI, a Texas-based company that manufactures DNA materials for use in labs around the world. That is, once injected, a DNA vaccine is likely to take effect more quickly and act more efficiently than other types of vaccines. As a result, VGXI states, a DNA vaccine will be highly "effective in stimulating antibody responses to attack infectious diseases as they enter the body, before they can infect cells, therefore acting as a preventive vaccine."[16]

Another advantage of DNA vaccines is that they will in many cases be able to target different mutations of a disease germ simultaneously, eliminating the need to develop a new vaccine for each mutation. Thus, VGXI explains, "the potential exists to develop a universal influenza vaccine to protect against both seasonal influenza strains as well as new influenza strains that cannot be known in advance and which present pandemic risk."[17]

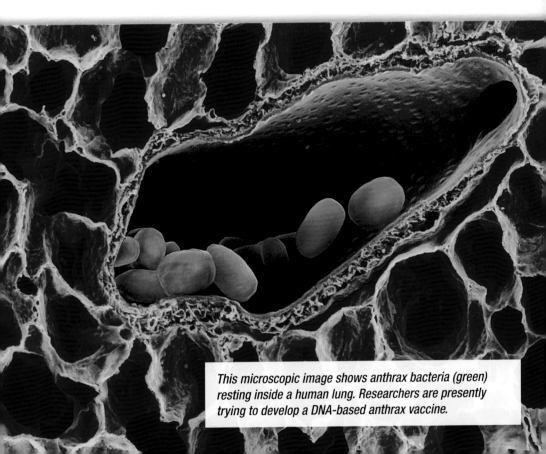

This microscopic image shows anthrax bacteria (green) resting inside a human lung. Researchers are presently trying to develop a DNA-based anthrax vaccine.

Still another likely benefit of DNA vaccines, experts say, is that they will be cost effective. Once the technology that underlies them is fully perfected, experts point out, manufacturing them will not require fancy and expensive new tools and equipment. Rather, making them will mainly utilize lab equipment and materials that are fairly standard and therefore already exist in labs worldwide.

Vectors That Carry Genetic Instructions

Another cutting edge vaccine that is currently under development in labs around the world uses DNA in a different way. Called a viral vector vaccine, it combines certain positive qualities of DNA vaccines with those of live attenuated vaccines. Unlike most vaccine approaches, the viral vector one does not introduce an antigen—that is, a germ or a piece or unit of a germ—into the body to stimulate an immune response. Instead, a viral vector vaccine induces a person's own cells to produce the antigen that will bring about immunity. This is accomplished by injecting genetic information into the body—in a sense, instructions to tell a person's cells how to make the antigen.

viral vector vaccine

A vaccine that induces a person's own cells to produce the antigen that will bring about immunity to a disease

To make such a vaccine for a specific illness—the target disease—researchers begin by selecting an existing virus to use as a vector, or carrier, of the genetic information. For instance, common vectors used in lab experiments to date have been the viruses that cause measles and the common cold. The vaccine does *not* utilize these germs in their normal form. Rather, first the researchers use genetic engineering techniques to strip away the genes that allow such a virus to cause disease symptoms.

Having rendered the virus harmless, the scientists next insert genetic instructions that "teach" the virus to make antigens of the target disease. Acting on those instructions, the person's cells now begin making the antigens. Almost immediately, the body's

Edible Genetic Vaccines

Among the many approaches to genetic vaccines currently under development around the world are an edible variety. Their purpose is to eliminate the need to inject them via needles, which some people—especially young children—find uncomfortable or even scary. The general approach in making edible vaccines is to combine the modified genes of a disease microbe with the genes of an edible plant. The vaccine recipient eats the doctored genes during a meal (or in pill form). Then the cells of that person's body detect the presence of the altered genetic materials. Assuming they constitute an attack by the disease in question, the body mounts the desired immune response.

Researchers are currently working with a number of plants to act as delivery vehicles for the vaccines. These include bananas, corn, tomatoes, potatoes, soybeans, and rice. One major advantage of making edible vaccines from these plants is that the distribution of such vaccines would be far simpler and cheaper. This is because local farmers in countries around the globe could grow the plants and give them to local lab technicians who are specially trained to create the vaccines. This would eliminate the need to import the vaccines from faraway destinations—a costly and time-consuming process.

immune system detects those antigens and mounts an attack on them, easily destroying them. The key to this entire process is that the immune system remembers those homemade invaders and will attack and destroy them no less fiercely if they ever appear again. Hence, the person is now immune to the targeted disease.

As has been the case with the development of many vaccines, researchers tend to first make versions that can be used to fight animal diseases. Vets administer them to various creatures, and if over time they prove safe and effective, the researchers advance to creating versions for humans. By 2021 close to a dozen viral vector vaccines were in use with various animals, and scientists expected human versions to be approved for use later in the 2020s.

The Long Road to mRNA Vaccines

Although researchers have worked for several decades on perfecting genetic vaccines that utilize various aspects of DNA, another major area of genetics—ribonucleic acid (RNA)—was long largely neglected. Only recently has the medical research community come around to utilizing RNA in the making of vaccines.

Along with DNA and proteins, RNA is one of the three most important physical factors in both heredity and the manufacture of the body's many different kinds of cells and tissues. Importantly, in the form of mRNA, RNA carries instructions from DNA molecules to the proteins that make up the bodily tissues. As early as the 1980s, some scientists realized that in theory one could use modified, or synthetic, mRNA molecules to manipulate the proteins in various ways. And perhaps one of these ways would involve making vaccines. Though tantalizing, the concept seemed closer to fantasy than reality. This is because it was well known that modified mRNA is extremely difficult to work with. Unlike natural mRNA, once modified by humans the molecule becomes unstable and is easily destroyed by various chemicals that normally exist in the blood.

One researcher, however, refused to give up on mRNA as a possible basis for vaccines. She is Hungarian-born American biochemist Katalin Karikó. During the 1990s she repeatedly experimented with mRNA. She was convinced that a modified version of it could be used to make specially tailored proteins and that those proteins could be employed to heal sick people. As medical reporters Damian Garde and Jonathan Saltzman put it, "If you could design your own mRNA, you could, in theory, hijack that process [of natural protein production] and create any protein you might desire [including] antibodies to vaccinate against infection."[18]

On paper, so to speak, this all seemed to make sense. But each time Karikó attempted to raise funding for major research into using mRNA to fight disease, government agencies and corporations turned her down. Their main worry, they told her, was that it would be too technically difficult and expensive to stop modified mRNA from being destroyed by the body before it could accomplish any healing.

Nevertheless, Karikó and a few like-minded researchers continued to experiment with mRNA using whatever limited funds they could raise. To their credit, little by little they eliminated the supposedly insurmountable difficulties of working with mRNA. As medical researcher Anthony Komaroff tells it, scientists "learned how to enclose the mRNA inside microscopically small capsules to protect it from being destroyed by chemicals in our blood." They also found ways to keep mRNA from creating "violent immune system reactions,"[19] which had long been another worry voiced by those who doubted that mRNA could be properly controlled.

Making the mRNA Vaccines

The courage, hard work, and sheer stubbornness of Karikó and her colleagues ultimately paid off. Almost no one could have predicted that, when COVID-19 suddenly started spreading around the globe in early 2020, mRNA vaccines would take the lead in the worldwide search for a cure. But that is in fact what occurred.

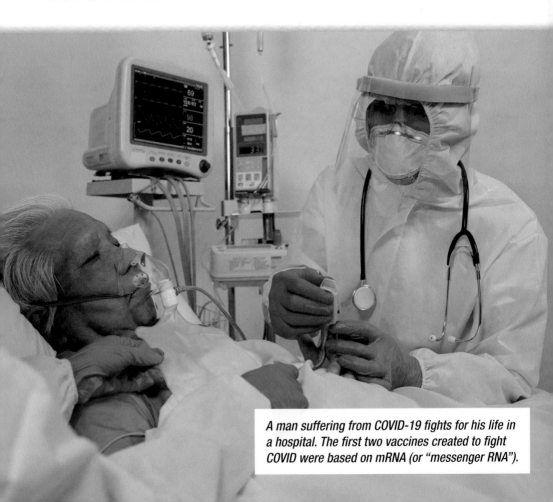

A man suffering from COVID-19 fights for his life in a hospital. The first two vaccines created to fight COVID were based on mRNA (or "messenger RNA").

That unexpected turn of events began in China in late 2019 and early 2020. Faced with COVID-19's emergence in the Chinese heartland, local researchers immediately went to work, determined to identify and map all the genes contained in the virus that causes the disease. In less than a month, they had managed to finish this incredibly complex task, which would have taken years to complete only a few decades earlier.

Wasting little time, the Chinese researchers published the information on the internet. This, they realized, would be an essential step in helping fellow scientists around the world get right to work on creating COVID-19 vaccines. This strategy worked with astounding speed. Less than half an hour after the information had been posted, dozens of scientists around the globe had downloaded it, and by the end of the day, every lab in the world that does vaccine research had it.

Most of those labs chose to utilize live attenuated, killed, or other traditional vaccines in the ensuing battle against the COVID-19 pandemic. However, Pfizer and Moderna both reasoned that, thanks to the recent advancements in working with mRNA, that substance now had the potential to compete with the others. Taking advantage of mRNA vaccine technology recently developed by Barney Graham and his team, both companies began making large batches of synthetic mRNA. They also isolated a key subunit in the COVID-19 virus, the so-called spike protein, and determined its exact genetic structure.

spike protein

The key subunit in the COVID-19 microbe that is used in making the mRNA COVID-19 vaccines

In modifying the mRNA molecules, the researchers programed them in such a way that they would give special instructions to the cells of a vaccinated person. Essentially, the message delivered by the mRNA tells those cells to manufacture small quantities of the COVID-19 spike protein. In turn, the person's immune system detects the protein, assumes it is a harmful invading germ, and produces the desired immune response to the disease.

Once the mRNA was encoded with the message, the researchers were ready to begin animal testing. Mice and monkeys were injected with the vaccine and shortly afterward were exposed to the virus. They not only proved immune to COVID-19 but also displayed no serious side effects. Human trials immediately followed, also with very positive results. Thus, less than a year after beginning their search for a vaccine, Pfizer and Moderna achieved spectacular success in record time.

Science's Ever-Expanding Chain

The triumphant scientists were quick to acknowledge that they could not have succeeded without the earlier work of researchers like Karikó and Graham. Science, they pointed out, is like an ever-expanding chain, with each new link building on the work that went into making the previous links. "Like every breakthrough," Komaroff explains, "the science behind the mRNA vaccine builds on many previous breakthroughs. . . . Every one of those past discoveries depended on the willingness of scientists to persist in pursuing their longshot dreams—often despite enormous skepticism and even ridicule—and the willingness of society to invest in their research."[20]

CHAPTER THREE

How Do We Know Vaccines Are Safe?

In April 2020 fifty-two-year-old Barry Colvin, a retired invest-ment manager living in White Plains, New York, read the lat-est news about the COVID-19 pandemic in his local newspa-per. Of particular interest was the fact that dozens of labs in the United States and around the world were hard at work on trying to develop vaccines that would prevent the spread of COVID-19. Moreover, two of the companies involved—Pfizer and Moderna—were attempting to make an mRNA-based vaccine. Colvin knew a little bit about how live and killed vac-cines worked. But he had never heard of mRNA, and what little the newspaper said about it fascinated him. "I started reading about the way the vaccines work," he later recount-ed, and "I was especially struck by the mRNA technique."[21]

At the time, Colvin wondered how, if the scientists did manage to create such a vaccine, they could be sure it was safe for him and other people worldwide. He received part of the answer to that question several weeks later when he read that some of the vaccine makers were looking for volunteers to join large-scale human trials of their vaccines. The article made the point that such trials constituted one of the chief ways that scientists determine the safety of such medicines. That fact sparked even more interest for Colvin. So he went online and learned about the many other ways that vaccines are tested for safety.

At the same time, Colvin came to realize that he himself could volunteer for such a trial and in that way help his fellow human beings. "I'm not a health care worker or an essential worker," he later pointed out. "So I can't contribute in that way." Nevertheless, he went on,

> I wanted to volunteer to try to expedite these efforts, especially in this era where people are nervous about vaccines. . . . My confidence in . . . the professionalism [of the scientists] has only strengthened during this experience. I was excited to participate in finding a way to prevent people from getting sick with this virus and getting our lives back to some level of normalcy.[22]

Another volunteer, Judy Stokes, a California-based retired health care writer in her sixties, also felt that taking part in a vaccine trial would be both constructive and patriotic. "As I considered joining [the trials]," she later recalled, "half of me was saying, Oh, you don't want to get involved in this! And the other half was telling me to do it. I was tired of being fearful and ineffectual during the pandemic. Volunteering was a positive step I could take, something I could do to hopefully move the vaccine development experience along."[23]

Some Trust Science; Others Do Not

Neither Colvin, Stokes, nor any of the thousands of other volunteers who took part in the COVID-19-related trials knew for sure whether the new vaccines they would be receiving were completely safe. Rather, they made an informed decision based partly on the fact that they trusted that the scientists had done the proper amount of research required to make vaccines in the first place. Also, the volunteers felt confident that the testing would not have reached the stage of human trials without having passed certain key scientific markers along the way.

The volunteers were also aware that, since vaccines' introduction in the late 1700s, these medicines have saved hundreds of millions of lives worldwide. Even a cursory glance at the history of medicine shows that vaccines have helped defeat a host of crippling and killer diseases, including smallpox, anthrax, and polio. Based on these facts, most of the volunteers in the COVID-19 vaccine trials wagered that taking part in the trials would likely be safe. "We . . . believe in science and medicine," remarked a husband and wife, both in their seventies, who volunteered. "I wanted to serve as a role model to suggest that others might believe [this way],"[24] the wife said when asked why she volunteered.

In stark contrast to the mindset of the volunteers is the attitude of a number of Americans who have far less confidence in science, and especially in vaccines. In some cases this negative view of vaccines stems from a lack of knowledge about how these medicines actually work, as well as the long, rich history of their

A doctor injects a patient with one of the vaccines developed to combat COVID-19. Before being approved, those remedies first underwent extensive human trials.

successes. Others who fall into this category, sometimes labeled "anti-vaxxers," are troubled by negative rumors that regularly circulate on the internet, particularly on social media. Largely baseless, such rumors suggest that vaccines are inherently unsafe and/or that they cause various adverse physical and mental conditions.

Animal Testing

Usually, those who are convinced that vaccines are or may be unsafe are also unaware of the extensive and strict safety tests that all new vaccine candidates undergo. Scientists working for the Centers for Disease Control and Prevention (CDC), the FDA, and hospitals and labs nationwide quite naturally want the public to know about those safety measures. So they routinely list and describe them in books, in journal articles, on the internet, and on other information platforms.

Scientists divide vaccine safety protocols into two major categories—pre-licensure, or those that happen before the FDA licenses a vaccine; and post-licensure, consisting of monitoring and tests accomplished after a vaccine has been licensed. During the extensive pre-licensure phase, the first line of defense against possible harmful effects of a new vaccine is animal testing. According to the CDC, "Vaccine development begins in the laboratory before any tests in animals or humans are done. If laboratory tests show that a vaccine has potential, it is usually tested in animals. If a vaccine is safe in animals, and studies suggest that it will be safe in people, clinical trials with volunteers are next."[25]

protocols

Procedural rules or regulations

Polio research conducted in the 1940s and 1950s provides one example of testing vaccines on animals prior to human trials. In the early years of studying that crippling ailment, researchers observed how it affected the nonhuman creatures that are physically the most like people—apes. Initial studies of some 9,000 monkeys and 150 chimpanzees were later followed by tests of two promising vaccines on various primates.

33

Vaccine Hesitancy

The first COVID-19 vaccines were administered in the United States in December 2020. Most Americans were ecstatic that vaccinations had begun, but many others were not. Public opinion polls conducted in late 2020 showed that a large percentage of Americans did not intend to get their shots. The Kaiser Family Foundation's poll discovered that 27 percent of adults had little or no faith in the vaccines. Gallup's survey put the proportion of citizens who would refuse to be vaccinated lower—11 percent—but another 10 percent said they were not sure.

The reasons given by many of the so-called vaccine-hesitant people are the same as those voiced about earlier vaccines. According to Renée DiResta of California's Stanford Internet Observatory, they include "the ingredients are toxic and unnatural; the vaccines are insufficiently tested; and the scientists who produce them are quacks and profiteers."

These concerns, which often circulate unchecked via social media, present a significant challenge for the medical community. That challenge, DiResta notes, "lies in countering anti-vaccine narratives with accurate information that can help instill confidence. . . . Avoiding confusion and misimpressions about vaccines from the beginning is of the greatest importance."

Renée DiResta, "Anti-Vaxxers Think This Is Their Moment," *The Atlantic*, December 2020. www.theatlantic.com.

Human Trials

For most vaccines, the human clinical trials occur in three phases, although more or fewer mass vaccination tests have happened on occasion. The Phase 1 trials focus mainly on safety and possible side effects. This stage usually involves a small number of people—anywhere from ten to one hundred volunteers.

If the Phase 1 trial produces the desired immune response and causes no serious side effects, the researchers move on to Phase 2. Most often this phase involves a few hundred to one thousand volunteers and focuses heavily on possible harmful side effects. If no particularly serious side effects are observed in Phase 2, the researchers move on to Phase 3. It features thousands of volunteers, and in some cases tens of thousands. Typically, it focuses most on how the size of the vaccine's dose relates to the immune response produced. That is, can a fairly small dose create the desired effect? Or will a bigger dose be required?

Still, Phase 3 also tries to answer the same question the other two phases did—namely, what are the side effects, if any? In this respect, Phase 3 is usually the most telling because it looks at a lot more subjects than the first two trials did. It is not unusual for certain rarer side effects not to appear in the first two trials but then show up in small numbers in Phase 3. This phenomenon has occurred in virtually all large-scale Phase 3 trials. The 1938 Phase 3 tests of the yellow fever vaccine on several thousand people, for example, revealed the possibility of side effects like joint pain, skin rash, and headaches. Similarly, possible side effects uncovered in the 1962 Phase 3 trials of the measles vaccine included nausea, vomiting, and mood changes. Almost always, the side effects revealed in Phase 3 trials are fairly rare. Even so, sometimes trials are paused to give the vaccine developer time to investigate those effects. If they are determined to be unrelated to the vaccine or pose no health threat, the trials can resume. If, however, the side effects prove to be serious, the trials can be halted.

Another way that the scientists test for such side effects in these trials is to give some of the volunteers a placebo—an injection

During human trials for new vaccines, health care workers giving the shots must follow strict guidelines set up by the FDA, the main headquarters of which is shown here.

FDA

U.S. Department of Health and Human Services
Food and Drug Administration

placebo

An injection containing a
harmless liquid instead of
the vaccine

containing a harmless liquid instead of the vaccine. For example, if some volunteers who got the vaccine and some who got the placebo both display a certain side effect, it may show that that effect was not caused by the vaccine. Conversely, if some who got the vaccine show a particular side effect and none who received the placebo show it, there is a strong indication that the vaccine caused that effect.

Throughout these trials, the scientists must follow strict safety measures mandated by the FDA, which keeps close tabs on the tests. According to the CDC, trained experts from the FDA try to

ensure the highest scientific and ethical standards. The results of the clinical trials are a part of FDA's evaluation to assess the safety and effectiveness of each vaccine. . . . [FDA] medical professionals carefully evaluate a wide range of information including results of studies on the vaccine's physical, chemical, and biological properties, as well as how it is manufactured, to ensure that it can be made consistently safe. . . . Only if a vaccine's benefits are found to outweigh its potential risks does the FDA grant a license for the vaccine, allowing it to be used by the public.[26]

An Elite Force of Medical Detectives

After the human trials are completed, if a new vaccine appears to be largely safe for the public, the FDA may grant it a license. However, safety testing always continues in the post-licensure stage. Scientists and FDA inspectors, who make up an elite force of medical detectives, monitor the vaccine for any harmful side effects that might not have emerged during the clinical trials. This extra screening is crucial because it could in theory show the existence of one or more rare side effects. Also, the clinical trials might not have included groups of people who might possess a higher risk of

Pfizer's Vaccine Authorized for Emergency Use

On November 29, 2020, the drugmaker Pfizer requested that the FDA grant emergency use authorization (EUA) for its COVID-19 vaccine. A little over three weeks later, on December 11, the FDA granted that request, which allowed Pfizer to move forward with mass production of the vaccine.

In announcing the decision, the director of the FDA's Center for Biologics Evaluation and Research, Peter Marks, cautioned that this step did not constitute full-fledged FDA approval of the vaccine. Rather, he explained, it was a temporary green light for the company to manufacture the vaccine. FDA officials have the power to grant EUA to any medical product they feel will serve the overall public good during a national emergency. Two main conditions must be met. First, the officials determine whether any existing FDA-approved alternatives could do the job just as well. Also, the FDA evaluates whether the clinical trials already conducted by the company in question have followed the high scientific standards the FDA regularly demands. If the officials decide that these conditions have been met, they may grant the company EUA.

side effects than average individuals. Examples of such groups are pregnant women and people who suffer from chronic medical conditions such as asthma, cystic fibrosis, obesity, or eating disorders.

If a new side effect shows up in this stage, a panel of medical experts called the Advisory Committee on Immunization Practices (ACIP) weighs in. If the panelists see that a significant percentage of the public might be adversely affected by the vaccine, they can recommend that the recently granted license be revoked. This rarely happens, because widespread side effects typically show up in the earlier stages of clinical trials. In that case, the panel typically upholds the license but orders that people in the higher-risk group not be given the vaccine. This is why a number of modern vaccines bear a warning that they should not be administered to pregnant women.

The ACIP panelists most often act on information gathered by a vaccine watchdog group called VAERS, which stands for Vaccine Adverse Event Reporting System. Overseen by the CDC and FDA, VAERS receives reports of unexpected vaccine side effects from doctors, nurses, vaccine manufacturers, and family members of people who have been vaccinated. When necessary, members of VAERS investigate these side effects and try to determine whether they are actually related to the vaccines in question. If they are, VAERS may recommend that the ACIP halt the use of a particular vaccine.

Although stopping the use of an already approved vaccine is not likely to happen very often, it did occur in a big way even before VAERS was created in 1990. In 1976, a new flu vaccine was licensed but then withdrawn after limited use. CDC investigators uncovered an unexpectedly high number of cases of Guillain-Barré syndrome (a condition in which the immune system attacks the nerves) in people who had received the vaccine. An estimated one in every one hundred thousand people who were vaccinated developed the syndrome, and fifty-three people died. Today, VAERS double-checks each new flu vaccine to ensure it will not cause that debilitating condition.

VAERS

The Vaccine Adverse Event Reporting System, which studies reports of unexpected vaccine side effects

A Complex Set of Safeguards

Still another layer of scrutiny and safety measures related to the creation and use of new vaccines consists of a VAERS-like surveillance system that monitors vaccine use on a national scale. That highly computerized system is called Post-Licensure Rapid Immunization Safety Monitoring, more often referred to as PRISM for short. All existing data about who is vaccinated for any disease in the United States goes to PRISM, which carefully stores and analyzes the information. "Because PRISM has access to historical information for over 100 million people, FDA is able to identify and analyze rare health outcomes that have previously been challenging to assess,"[27] the US Department of Health and Human Services states on one of its websites.

Pregnant women are often initially excluded from human trials of vaccines to ensure that their unborn children are not adversely affected by those substances.

A clear example of a rare health outcome uncovered by PRISM occurred during 2010 to 2012. The system initially compared several medical studies that involved rotavirus, which causes severe diarrhea in children. Data stored in PRISM indicated that a rare intestinal condition might be linked to use of the US-licensed vaccine for rotavirus in some subgroups of children. When this was confirmed, the FDA added a warning to the vaccine's label that allows doctors to make sure that high-risk children do not receive it.

Thus, a complex set of safeguards exist to monitor vaccines both before and after they are licensed. Numerous studies have shown that although all vaccines have side effects, the vast majority are minor, and the benefits of a vaccine far outweigh the risk of those effects. Moreover, the system effectively weeds out any rare instances of more serious side effects. These safeguards inspire a majority of Americans to have confidence in the safety of the vaccines. This confidence is part of what motivated Judy Stokes to join the COVID-19 clinical trials in 2020. Not long after taking part, she said, "This experience has given me a real appreciation of science and how medicine moves carefully to make sure it works safely and effectively. I'm glad I entered the trial. . . . Creating an effective vaccine can help us all return to the things we value."[28]

CHAPTER FOUR

Vaccine Success Stories

In early 1960, after examining the results of a recent vaccine experiment, thirty-seven-year-old English veterinary scientist Walter Plowright was pleased with what he saw. He now knew that he was close to producing a vaccine that could potentially rid the world of one of the worst diseases ever to affect humanity. More than a decade earlier, he had decided to devote his career to finding a vaccine to vanquish some deadly ailment. While trying to choose one, he considered that some diseases infected only people, others attacked only animals, while still others plagued both humans and animals.

Eventually, Plowright settled on rinderpest, a lethal malady that for thousands of years had killed millions of cattle, sheep, goats, and other creatures that people depend on for food, milk, clothing, and much more. Thousands of humans died of starvation every year, he realized, because rinderpest destroyed huge numbers of these animals. Thereafter, he spent nearly every waking hour of every week, month, and year working on a possible vaccine for the disease, sometimes spending long periods studying it in Kenya, Nigeria, and other nations where it took an awful annual toll.

By 1962 Plowright had managed to perfect his vaccine, and he and other scientists immediately began distributing it to farmers around the world. Small-scale successes in some areas continued to occur until the 1990s, when the Food and Agriculture Organization of the United Nations (FAO) backed the effort on an even bigger scale. That effort paid off with one of the greatest triumphs of modern science. In May 2011, UN officials announced that, after the elimination of smallpox in 1980, rinderpest had become the second deadly disease that scientists had eradicated from the face of the earth.

> **rinderpest**
>
> A disease that affected cattle, sheep, goats, and other animals until it was declared eradicated in 2011

One high-placed medical authority stated, "It's a major breakthrough, not only for science, but also for the cooperation policies amongst international organizations and with the international community as a whole."[29] That same week, Ann Tutwiler, deputy director of the FAO, said about rinderpest, "With the eradication of the disease in live animals, livestock production around the globe has become safer and the livelihoods of millions of livestock farmers are less at risk."[30] Tragically, Plowright was unable to witness the final success of his life's work because he had passed away the year before. But his name remains high on the list of the scientific heroes whose vaccines changed the world for the better.

An Earthshaking Question

Plowright was neither the first nor the last vaccine hero to save untold millions of lives, both human and nonhuman. The first, and perhaps still the most legendary, of those pioneers was French chemist Louis Pasteur. In 1854, at age thirty-two, he had not yet gained any major notoriety in scientific circles and made it known that he was available to accept chemistry-related assignments on a for-hire basis. That same year a group of French winemakers approached him. They explained that they very much desired to earn larger profits but that a major obstacle impeded them—namely, that wine naturally tended to spoil under certain conditions while aging. If Pasteur could find a way to either slow that process or eliminate it, they said, they would reward him quite handsomely.

Eager to find the answer to such a fundamental and long-standing scientific mystery, the young chemist threw himself into the project. It did not take him long to declare that he had found the answer. After a thorough examination of the evidence, he discovered that microscopic bacteria caused wine to spoil. Scientists did know of the existence of bacteria and other kinds of germs at the time. However, the general consensus was that those tiny organisms played no important role in nature and were almost certainly harmless. Pasteur had agreed with that assumption before his study of wine spoilage. But now it occurred to him that if germs could make wine spoil, maybe they could harm plants, animals, and people too.

The more he thought about it, the more Pasteur worried about microbes and what they might be capable of. Could they actually be the principal cause of the various diseases that had visited

In 1896, farmworkers in South Africa struggle to help a cow suffering from the devastating animal disease rinderpest. A successful vaccine for that malady appeared in 1962.

misery on humanity since the dawn of time? he wondered. As time went on, he increasingly devoted more and more effort to answering that question.

Eventually, various clues made Pasteur certain that germs were indeed the culprits behind disease. "The cause of transmissible, contagious and infectious diseases resides essentially and uniquely in the presence of microorganisms,"[31] he concluded. One way he sought to confirm that conclusion was to search for a way to use a specific disease microbe to make a vaccine. In this regard, he built on the work of earlier researchers who had shown that inoculating a person with germs associated with a given disease seemed to stimulate immunity to that ailment.

The Miracle at Melun

Among Pasteur's earliest immunity experiments were studies of an animal disease, chicken cholera. First he cultured the cholera germs and injected them into chickens in the lab. In time he observed that as the germs aged they became weaker and less harmful to the chickens. On a hunch, Pasteur injected some chickens with the weakened germs and noted that they did not contract the disease, as most people assumed would happen. Surprised, he and his assistants gave the birds full-strength chicken cholera germs, and they still remained disease-free. Clearly, the researchers realized, not only were the weakened germs too weak to cause the disease, they also made the chickens immune to it. "Ah, this is wonderful!" Pasteur exclaimed. "The old culture protected the hens against the virulent [lethal] germ. Hens can be vaccinated against chicken cholera!"[32]

Daringly, Pasteur decided to try applying these discoveries to anthrax, a terrifying disease that infects both animals and people. He and his helpers cultured anthrax microbes, weakened them by adding heat, and injected them into lab animals. Excitedly, they saw that, as they had hoped, the creatures displayed immunity to anthrax. Pasteur was shocked, however, when other scientists were skeptical that such a thing could be possible. In particular, the

The First Viral Vaccine

One advantage Louis Pasteur had when working with cholera and anthrax was that with his microscope he could easily see the germs that cause those ailments. Both diseases are bacterial, and bacteria are fairly large as microbes go. When trying to make a vaccine for rabies, however, Pasteur dealt with a germ so tiny that it was invisible in the most powerful microscopes of his day. Though frustrated, he was neither stumped nor deterred by that disadvantage. Pasteur rightly reasoned that the rabies germs were invisible because they were much smaller than bacteria.

Years later, other scientists named those tinier microorganisms viruses. Despite his inability to see the rabies virus, Pasteur was able to weaken them and use them to make a vaccine for the disease. Initially, he conducted clinical trials on more than one hundred dogs, all of which became immune to rabies. The first human test occurred in March 1885 when the mother of a nine-year-old boy implored Pasteur to save her son. The boy, Joseph Meister, had been bitten by a rabid dog. The rabies vaccine Pasteur had created succeeded in making young Joseph immune to the disease, opening the way for the development of vaccines to defeat viral diseases.

widely respected French veterinarian Hippolyte Rossignol scoffed at Pasteur's conclusions and belittled Pasteur himself. Rossignol also challenged him to prove his hypothesis in a public demonstration.

Pasteur accepted the challenge, and the history-making event occurred in May 1881 in a field at Melun, a village south of Paris. A large crowd of spectators looked on as Pasteur and his assistants vaccinated twenty-five sheep with the new anthrax vaccine. Beside them stood another twenty-five sheep that remained unvaccinated. Several days later, the crowd returned to see Pasteur inject all fifty sheep with live, deadly anthrax germs.

On June 2 the biggest crowd yet gathered to watch the final stage of the test. That morning, Pasteur awoke in Paris and prepared to go to Melun. Before getting on the train, however, he received an emergency telegram. It was from none other than Rossignol, and it ended with the words "Stunning success!"[33] Hurrying to Melun, Pasteur exited the train to find himself the focus of a thunderous ovation from thousands of people of all walks of life. As some of them patted his back and called him a miracle worker, he made his way to the sheep. Twenty-two of the unvaccinated ones lay dead, and the other three were nearly expired, while all twenty-five of the vaccinated ones stood very much alive and perfectly healthy. At that moment Rossignol appeared, heartily embraced Pasteur, and apologized for doubting him.

Mounting an Assault on Polio

Four years later, in July 1885, Pasteur followed up on his groundbreaking anthrax vaccine by introducing an effective vaccine for rabies. By the close of that year, many hundreds of people worldwide who had been bitten by rabid creatures and otherwise would surely have died had been saved. Thereafter, a small army of researchers stepped up the search for vaccines targeting other deadly maladies. Thanks to their tireless efforts, a typhoid vaccine emerged in 1899; a cholera vaccine in 1911; a yellow fever vaccine in 1938; a vaccine for whooping cough in 1939; and the first widely distributed influenza vaccine in 1945.

These and other successful vaccines introduced in the twentieth century saved the lives of millions of people. Yet a great many debilitating diseases remained threats to humanity,

French scientist Louis Pasteur vaccinates sheep against anthrax at Melun, France, south of Paris. The experiment was a resounding success.

so scientists continued their assaults on them in the 1950s, 1960s, and 1970s. Of those efforts, perhaps the most famous and dramatic was the conquest of poliomyelitis, most often called polio for short. That illness, which can cause severe paralysis, most often strikes children younger than fourteen (although adults can also get it). During the 1940s some years witnessed tens of thousands of new cases, causing millions of parents to fear for their children's safety.

Perhaps because the disease so often targeted young people, a growing number of scientists were inspired to seek a vaccine to combat it. A great deal of money was needed to fund that effort, so in 1938 President Franklin D. Roosevelt founded the National Foundation for Infantile Paralysis, later more informally known as the March of Dimes. Roosevelt had a personal interest in polio because he had become one of its victims in 1921. Thereafter, as governor of New York and US president, he required braces, crutches, and sometimes a wheelchair to get around.

formaldehyde

A powerful chemical that researcher Jonas Salk used to weaken polio viruses to make his polio vaccine

As the search for a polio vaccine proceeded in numerous labs nationwide, one young scientist quickly emerged as the leading polio researcher. In 1948 the March of Dimes hired thirty-four-year-old Jonas Salk to study and hopefully defeat the disease. While Salk began examining the various strains of polio, he gathered a team of more than fifty top immunologists, biologists, and chemists. The team eventually decided that the safest approach was to make a killed vaccine that would create immunity to all the polio strains. To kill the polio viruses, they employed the powerful chemical formaldehyde.

The World Held Its Breath
Numerous lab experiments and tests, including vaccine trials on hundreds of monkeys, ensued in the four years that followed. Fi-

Vaccines That Battle Deadly Meningitis

Meningitis (or meningococcal disease), which can be caused variously by a virus, bacterium, or fungus, is a serious infection of the lining of the brain and spinal cord. Common symptoms include fever, stiff neck, headaches, feelings of confusion, and vomiting. For reasons still not totally understood, some people die from the disease, while others merely carry it without getting sick. Roughly 1,400 to 2,800 cases of meningitis occur annually in the United States, a figure that was much higher before the introduction of meningitis vaccines. Case numbers remain a good deal higher in several nations in sub-Saharan Africa. That area witnesses as many as 200,000 cases of the disease each year. Smaller hot spots for meningitis exist in Asia and South America. Globally, about 300,000 people die from the disease annually. That is down from more than 450,000 deaths per year in the early 1990s, a reduction attributed in large part to the introduction of vaccines designed to combat the ailment. The first vaccine for meningitis appeared in the 1970s but proved only moderately effective. Far more successful vaccines came in 2005 and 2010 and are now the preferred prevention methods for people aged two to fifty-five.

nally, in early 1953 the researchers felt the time had come to test the vaccine on people. Salk did not want to risk administering it widely to the public before some initial human trials, and he boldly began those tests by injecting himself and the members of his immediate family. This and a few bigger trials all produced positive results, so Salk advocated moving forward with a much larger-scale trial—the public vaccination of some 1.8 million schoolchildren ages six to nine. That dramatic effort began in April 1954.

Overseen by the widely respected physician Thomas Francis Jr. of the University of Michigan, a team of experts monitored the test and carefully analyzed the results. The world in a sense held its collective breath in anticipation during the months in which Francis's team did its vital job. Finally, on April 12, 1955, Francis made global front page headlines when he announced that Salk's vaccine was "safe, effective, and potent."[34]

Mass production of the vaccine and a huge vaccination program swiftly followed. To call this effort successful would be an understatement, for it was truly a triumph of the first order. By 1961, a mere six years after the vaccine's approval, US medical

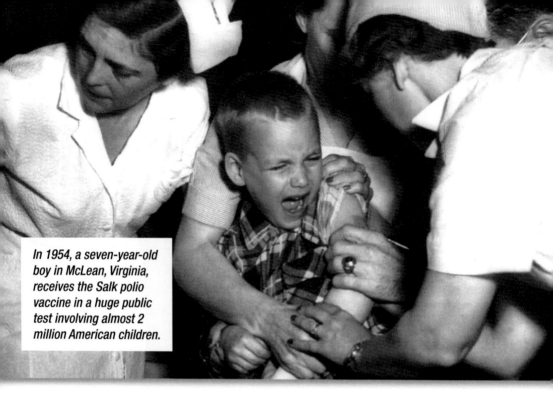

In 1954, a seven-year-old boy in McLean, Virginia, receives the Salk polio vaccine in a huge public test involving almost 2 million American children.

authorities reported the occurrence of only five hundred cases of polio, less than 1 percent of the yearly number in the early 1950s. Physician and science writer Meredith Wadman writes that Salk's work and that of Albert Sabin, who created a second successful polio vaccine, were part of "a heroic quest" by scientists "driven and well-funded."[35] Thanks to these and other hardworking researchers, she says, the world was safer than it had ever been from a long list of frightening diseases.

Recent Success Stories

Although they have beaten back ancient sicknesses such as anthrax, cholera, and polio, vaccines have also proved successful against emerging, previously unknown diseases. The situation with COVID-19 is an apt example. Another well-known recent example is Ebola, a highly contagious malady that causes severe fever, diarrhea, liver failure, and usually death. The firstknown cases appeared in western Africa in 1976. Later, much bigger epidemics took place in the 1990s and 2013–2014, with more than twenty-nine thousand cases reported in that third outbreak.

In their efforts to find an Ebola vaccine, scientists first studied it in detail and determined that it was originally an animal disease. It circulated among bats and other wild creatures for an unknown number of years before making the leap to humans in the second half of the twentieth century. Several labs in various nations sought a cure, but a Canadian company was the first to develop one in 2016—a DNA subunit vaccine.

VSV

The abbreviation of vesicular stomatitis virus, a disease of cattle, pigs, and a number of other animal species

To make the vaccine, researchers began by isolating a protein on the surface of a germ that causes the animal disease designated VSV. That illness was chosen because it does not cause infections in humans; thus, injecting VSV microbes into people causes no ill effects. After locating the protein, the scientists removed it and replaced it with one of the proteins in the Ebola virus. Because that protein is harmless to humans, the researchers hoped it would trigger an immune reaction to Ebola.

Although that approach worked, certain technical difficulties kept the vaccine from being approved right away. Eventually, however, the large pharmaceutical company Merck took over the project and overcame the last roadblocks. In December 2019 Merck announced that the vaccine, called Ervebo, was effective, and more than one hundred thousand people—mostly in Africa—were vaccinated in the few months that followed. Realizing that the vaccine had saved many lives, the Merck scientist who had overseen Ervebo's development stated, "We are thrilled and we are proud!"[36]

Those few and simple words hardly do justice to the enormous good that vaccines have wrought for humankind. Today research continues in hopes that these medical marvels might someday work against cancer and other terrible maladies. Summing up the incredible story of vaccines, Britain's National Health Service calls them "one of the greatest breakthroughs in modern medicine. No other medical intervention has done more to save lives and improve quality of life."[37]

The Challenges of Vaccine Distribution

The widely hailed miracle of the development of COVID-19 vaccines represented the first enormous challenge of this effort, but not the last. By early December 2020, two vaccines (made by Pfizer and Moderna) were ready for distribution, and dozens of others were in clinical trials and almost ready. This raised the hopes of Americans—and indeed, people around the world. By late December, however, those hopes were fast fading in US cities and towns. The federal government had promised to give 20 million Americans their first shots by December 31, but when that date passed, fewer than 3 million people had been vaccinated. Moreover, thereafter distribution of the vaccines fell steadily further behind. A December 2020 *New York Times* editorial called it "an astonishing failure" caused by "poor coordination at the federal level, combined with a lack of funding and support for state and local entities." The editorial continued, "In the end, vaccines are a lot like other public health measures. Their success depends on their implementation."[38]

A Very Different Era

Distribution problems with vaccines have happened before. The initially poor implementation of Jonas Salk's polio vaccine in the 1950s is an example. When the vaccine finally received authorization for widescale use, many Americans expected to be able to immediately get their children immunized. That did not happen, however, because no distribution system had been set up for mass vaccinations. At the time, the federal government had only a limited role in vaccine research and distribution, so this effort was ultimately organized and funded mostly by private charities. As a result, it was not until the early 1960s that the vast majority of US children were immunized against polio.

Today the federal government, through its various agencies, oversees public health. Through its partnerships with universities and biotech companies, it coordinated and funded a lot of the COVID-19 vaccine research. The federal government was also thought to be orchestrating mass production and distribution of those vaccines. But that did not happen as expected. By January 2021, newly-elected President Joe Biden took office, it became clear that vaccine production had fallen far short of the early goals. Pfizer and Moderna had each promised to produce 100 million doses by March 1. But in late January they were each making only about 4.3 million doses per week, not nearly enough to meet their stated goals. Furthermore, there appeared to be no national plan for vaccine distribution. The federal government had shifted responsibility for distributing vaccines to individual states, cities, and counties. That "left many local health officials overwhelmed," Politico reporter Dan Diamond writes, "saying that they didn't receive sufficient funding or resources to handle the work of administering doses."[39]

Valuable Lessons

Shortly before taking office, Joe Biden announced his goal of vaccinating 100 million Americans for COVID-19 in his first hundred days in the White House. By February 19, 2021, with twenty of those one hundred days elapsed, about 33 million Americans had received at least one of the two shots required to achieve immunity. Part of the reason for this initial success was that on January

Health care workers administer the Pfizer COVID-19 vaccine to senior citizens in Groveland, Florida, in January 2021. The individual states were initially overwhelmed by the task of vaccinating the public.

22, two days after assuming office, Biden invoked the Defense Production Act (DPA), an emergency measure available to the federal government. Designed to have private companies assist the government in producing items the country badly needs, it works in the following way: The Defense Department places an order with a company—for instance for glass vials for a vaccine or for syringes to administer it. The company is obliged to fill that order right away, before it fills any others. This is because when the DPA is in place the federal government legally has priority over private enterprises.

Biden also ordered the creation of at least one hundred new federally sponsored vaccination sites around the nation. That increased the number from 175 to 275. In addition, he began arrangements for several thousand National Guard troops to assist with the operation of those federal sites.

However long it takes to vaccinate everyone, experts point out that both the failures and successes associated with vaccine development provide valuable lessons. How ordinary citizens deal with a pandemic and how vaccines can be more efficiently distributed to fight it require improvement, says Oxford University scholar Dennis J. Snower. Government, society, and businesses can all learn from today's mistakes and thereby be better prepared for future pandemics, he says. "The pandemic shows us that the goals of all these domains must always [be] the same: contributing to the fulfillment of human needs and purposes."[40]

Introduction: A Moon Landing for Modern Medicine

1. Quoted in Beth JoJack, "How Has the Pandemic Influenced Our Relationship with Nature?," Medical News Today, 2021. www.medicalnewstoday.com.
2. Quoted in Eric J. Rubin et al., "ARS-CoV-2 Vaccination—an Ounce (Actually, Much Less) of Prevention," *New England Journal of Medicine*, December 21, 2020. www.nejm.org.
3. Quoted in Rubin et al., "ARS-CoV-2 Vaccination—an Ounce (Actually, Much Less) of Prevention."
4. Quoted in JoJack, "How Has the Pandemic Influenced Our Relationship with Nature?"
5. Quoted in JoJack, "How Has the Pandemic Influenced Our Relationship with Nature?"

Chapter One: How the Vaccine Workhorses Fight Disease

6. Quoted in Bismarck Swangin, "Yemen's First-Ever Cholera Vaccination Program," UNICEF, 2018. www.unicef.org.
7. Quoted in Swangin, "Yemen's First-Ever Cholera Vaccination Program."
8. World Health Organization, "COVID-19 Vaccines," 2021. www.who.int.
9. American Academy of Allergy, Asthma, and Immunology, "Vaccines: The Myths and the Facts," 2019. www.aaaai.org.
10. Mayo Clinic, "Rabies," 2021. www.mayoclinic.org.
11. Pan American Health Organization and World Health Organization, "Epidemiological Update—Diphtheria in the Americas—Summary of the Situation—10 May 2019," ReliefWeb, May 10, 2019. https://reliefweb.int.
12. Quoted in World Health Organization, "Malaria Vaccine Pilot Launched in Malawi," April 23, 2019. www.who.int.
13. Quoted in World Health Organization, "Malaria Vaccine Pilot Launched in Malawi."

Chapter Two: Vaccines on the Cutting Edge

14. Carolyn Y. Johnson, "A Gamble Pays Off in 'Spectacular Success': How the Leading Coronavirus Vaccines Made It to the Finish Line," *Washington Post*, December 6, 2020. www.washingtonpost.com.
15. Johnson, "A Gamble Pays Off in 'Spectacular Success.'"
16. VGXI, "What Are DNA Vaccines?," March 2, 2012. https://vgxii .com.
17. VGXI, "What Are DNA Vaccines?"
18. Damian Garde and Jonathan Saltzman, "The Story of mRNA: How a Once-Dismissed Idea Became a Leading Technology in the Covid Vaccine Race," Stat, November 10, 2020. www.statnews.com.
19. Anthony Komaroff, "Why Are mRNA Vaccines So Exciting?," *Harvard Health Blog*, Harvard Medical School, December 10, 2020. www.health.harvard.edu.
20. Komaroff, "Why Are mRNA Vaccines So Exciting?"

Chapter Three: How Do We Know Vaccines Are Safe?

21. Quoted in Stacey Colino, "Why I Volunteered: Inspiring Stories of COVID-19 Vaccine Trial Participants," AARP, December 8, 2020. www.aarp.org.
22. Quoted in Colino, "Why I Volunteered."
23. Quoted in Colino, "Why I Volunteered."
24. Quoted in Colino, "Why I Volunteered."
25. Centers for Disease Control and Prevention, "Ensuring the Safety of Vaccines in the United States," June 27, 2018. www.cdc.gov.
26. Centers for Disease Control and Prevention, "Ensuring the Safety of Vaccines in the United States."
27. US Department of Health and Human Services, "Advances in the Science, Surveillance, and Safety of Vaccines," March 27, 2016. www.hhs.gov.
28. Quoted in Colino, "Why I Volunteered."

Chapter Four: Vaccine Success Stories

29. Quoted in Lisa Schnirring, "OIE Declares Rinderpest Eradicated," University of Minnesota Center for Infectious Disease Research and Policy, May 25, 2011. www.cidrap.umn.edu.
30. Quoted in Schnirring, "OIE Declares Rinderpest Eradicated."
31. Quoted in Kendall A. Smith, "Louis Pasteur: The Father of Immunology?," *Frontiers in Immunology*, March 4, 2012. www.ncbi.nlm.nih.gov.

32. Quoted in René Valery-Radot, *The Life of Pasteur*, trans. R.L Devonshire. Charleston, SC: Bibliolife, 2008, p. 120.
33. Quoted in John S. Avery, *Science and Society*. Hackensack, NJ: World Scientific, 2017, p. 192.
34. Quoted in Office of the President, University of Michigan, "About Thomas Francis, Jr.," 2021. https://president.umich.edu.
35. Meredith Wadman, *The Vaccine Race: Science, Politics, and the Human Costs of Defeating Disease*. New York: Viking, 2017, pp. 7–8.
36. Quoted in Helen Branswell, "'Against All Odds': The Inside Story of How Scientists Across Three Continents Produced an Ebola Vaccine," Stat, January 7, 2020. www.statnews.com.
37. Quoted in From Antiquity to the Stars, "Statements in Support of Vaccines from Major Science and Medical Organizations," August 21, 2015. https://fromantiquitytothestars.wordpress.com.

Epilogue: The Challenges of Vaccine Distribution

38. *New York Times* Editorial Board, "We Came All This Way to Let Vaccines Go Bad in the Freezer?," *New York Times*, December 31, 2020. www.nytimes.com.
39. Dan Diamond, "The Crash Landing of 'Operation Warp Speed,'" Politico, January 17, 2021. www.politico.com.
40. Dennis J. Snower, "Fundamental Lessons from the COVID-19 Pandemic," Global Solutions, 2020. www.global-solutions-initiative.org.

Coronavirus Disease (COVID-19), US Department of Labor
www.osha.gov/SLTC/covid-19

This excellent site contains numerous links leading to a wide range of information about COVID-19, including medical facts, symptoms, control and prevention, how workers can avoid contracting the virus, the importance of wearing masks, and much more.

The History of Vaccines, College of Physicians of Philadelphia
www.historyofvaccines.org

Philadelphia's famed College of Physicians has here put together an enormously informative, accurate, and useful site about vaccines, including a comprehensive timeline and links to numerous relevant articles and fact boxes.

Immunizations, American Academy of Pediatrics (AAP)
www.aap.org/en-us/advocacy-and-policy/aap-health-initiatives
/immunizations/Pages/Immunizations-home.aspx

The immunization section of the AAP website provides a wealth of information about children's vaccination programs, policies, and schedules, along with information about vaccines for COVID-19, HPV, and other ailments.

Vaccine Awareness and Research (CVAR), Texas Children's Hospital
www.texaschildrens.org/departments/vaccine-awareness-and-research-cvar

Texas Children's Hospital, located in Houston, Texas, is dedicated to creating a healthy, successful future for children in the United States and around the world, partly by promoting education and research into the latest vaccines. The site offers up-to-date information about COVID-19 and the latest vaccines for it.

Vaccines and Immunization, World Health Organization (WHO)
www.who.int/topics/vaccines/en

WHO provides this informative site, which contains numerous links to facts on current vaccine research and development, vaccine safety issues, information about vaccines for children and infants, and much more.

Books

Craig E. Blohm, *The Search for a COVID-19 Vaccine*. San Diego, CA: ReferencePoint, 2021.

Tara Haelle, *Vaccination Investigation: The History and Science of Vaccines*. Minneapolis, MN: Twentieth-Century, 2018.

Michelle Harris, *Vaccines: The Truth Behind the Debates*. New York: Lucent, 2019.

Peter J. Hotez, *Preventing the Next Pandemic.* Baltimore: Johns Hopkins University Press, 2021.

Pete Schauer, *AIDS and Other Killer Viruses and Pandemics*. Farmington Hills, MI: Greenhaven, 2018.

Internet Sources

Association of the British Pharmaceutical Industry, "What Does the Future of Vaccines Look Like?," 2021. www.abpi.org.uk.

Biography, "Louis Pasteur," June 12, 2020. www.biography.com.

Centers for Disease Control and Prevention, "COVID-19 Vaccine: Helps Protect You from Getting COVID-19," February 8, 2021. www.cdc.gov.

Centers for Disease Control and Prevention, "Ensuring the Safety of Vaccines in the United States," June 27, 2018. www.cdc.gov.

College of Physicians of Philadelphia, "Careers in Vaccine Research," January 10, 2018. https://ftp.historyofvaccines.org.

College of Physicians of Philadelphia, "Ebola Virus Disease and Ebola Vaccines," January 10, 2018. https://ftp.historyofvaccines.org.

Dan Diamond, "The Crash Landing of 'Operation Warp Speed,'" Politico, January 17, 2021. www.politico.com.

Adam Edelman et al., "Biden to Deploy FEMA, National Guard as Part of National Vaccination Plan," NBC News, January 15, 2021. www.nbcnews.com.

Damian Garde and Jonathan Saltzman, "The Story of mRNA: How a Once-Dismissed Idea Became a Leading Technology in the Covid Vaccine Race," Stat, November 10, 2020. www.statnews.com.

National Cancer Institute, "Immunotherapy to Treat Cancer," September 24, 2019. www.cancer.gov.

New York Times Editorial Board, "We Came All This Way to Let Vaccines Go Bad in the Freezer?," *New York Times*, December 31, 2020. www.nytimes.com.

US Department of Health and Human Services, "Vaccine Safety," 2020. www.vaccines.gov.

INDEX

PICTURE CREDITS

Cover: DC Studio/Shutterstock

6: HRAUN/Shutterstock.com
10: Associated Press
14: Science Source
17: Associated Press
21: A. Barrington Brown/Science Source
23: Dennis Kunkel Microscopy/Science Source
27: Pordee Aomboo/Shutterstock
32: Dragana Gordic/Shutterstock
35: JHVEPhoto/Shutterstock
39: Coffeemill/Shutterstock
42: Look and Learn/Illustrated Papers Collection/
     Bridgeman Images
45: Tarker/Bridgeman Images
48: CSU Archives/Everett Collection/ Bridgeman Images
52: Associated Press